50 Kitchen Alchemy Recipes

By: Kelly Johnson

Table of Contents

- Garlic Honey Ferment
- Fire Cider
- Homemade Vanilla Extract
- Lacto-Fermented Hot Sauce
- Kombucha
- Sourdough Starter
- Fermented Lemon Preserves
- Kimchi
- Sauerkraut
- Pickled Red Onions
- Black Garlic
- Infused Olive Oils
- Herb-Infused Vinegars
- Fermented Cashew Cheese
- Miso Paste
- Soy Sauce Fermentation
- Homemade Yogurt
- Kefir
- Golden Milk Paste

- Bone Broth
- Mushroom Broth
- Fire Roasted Salsa
- Fermented Salsa
- Homemade Ghee
- Herb Butter Blends
- Chive Blossom Vinegar
- Dandelion Wine
- Elderberry Syrup
- Mead
- Infused Spirits (Rosemary Vodka, etc.)
- Homemade Bitters
- Fermented Ketchup
- Homemade Worcestershire Sauce
- Ginger Bug Starter
- Apple Cider Vinegar
- Herbal Simple Syrups
- Chaga Tea
- Reishi Mushroom Tincture
- Beet Kvass
- Pickled Garlic

- Sweet Fermented Rice (Amazake)
- Smoked Salt
- Fermented Nut Milk
- Wild Yeast Starter
- Herbal Gummy Bears
- Preserved Egg Yolks
- Infused Honey (Lavender, Cinnamon, etc.)
- Turmeric Pickles
- Lemon Balm Oxymel
- Fermented Carrot Sticks

Garlic Honey Ferment

Ingredients:

- 1 cup raw garlic cloves (peeled)
- 1 cup raw honey (preferably local and unpasteurized)

Instructions:

1. **Prepare the Garlic**: Peel the garlic cloves and lightly crush them with a knife to help release their juices.
2. **Fill the Jar**: Place the garlic cloves in a clean, sterilized glass jar.
3. **Add the Honey**: Pour the raw honey over the garlic until fully submerged.
4. **Fermentation Process**:
   - Seal the jar loosely (to allow gases to escape).
   - Store in a cool, dark place at room temperature.
   - Every day for the first week, open the jar to release built-up gases and stir or rotate the jar to keep the garlic covered.
5. **Wait & Enjoy**: Let it ferment for at least **2-4 weeks** (flavor deepens over time).
6. **Storage**: Keep in a cool, dark place or refrigerate for longer shelf life. The honey will become thinner as the garlic releases juices.

How to Use:

- Eat a clove daily for immune support.
- Drizzle the infused honey over toast, cheese, or roasted vegetables.
- Add to marinades, dressings, or teas.

Fire Cider

Ingredients:

- 1/2 cup grated fresh ginger
- 1/2 cup grated fresh horseradish
- 1 small onion, diced
- 10 cloves garlic, minced
- 2 jalapeños, sliced
- 1 lemon, sliced
- 2 tbsp turmeric powder or fresh turmeric, grated
- 1/2 tsp black pepper
- 2 tbsp raw honey (optional)
- 2 cups raw apple cider vinegar

Instructions:

1. Add all ingredients except honey to a sterilized glass jar.
2. Pour apple cider vinegar over until fully submerged.
3. Seal the jar with a plastic lid or cover with parchment paper before sealing with a metal lid.
4. Shake daily and store in a cool, dark place for 3-4 weeks.
5. Strain and mix in honey to taste.
6. Store in the fridge and take 1-2 tbsp daily.

Homemade Vanilla Extract

Ingredients:

- 6 vanilla beans
- 1 cup vodka, bourbon, or rum

Instructions:

1. Split vanilla beans lengthwise and place them in a sterilized jar.
2. Pour alcohol over the beans, ensuring they are fully submerged.
3. Seal and store in a dark place for at least 8 weeks (longer for a stronger flavor).
4. Shake occasionally. Use in baking or as a flavor enhancer.

Lacto-Fermented Hot Sauce

Ingredients:

- 2 cups chili peppers (any variety)
- 4 cloves garlic
- 1 tbsp sea salt
- 2 cups non-chlorinated water
- 1 tbsp sugar (optional, for fermentation boost)

Instructions:

1. Chop chili peppers and garlic, then place in a sterilized jar.
2. Dissolve salt in water and pour over peppers.
3. Weigh down ingredients to keep submerged.
4. Cover loosely and ferment at room temp for 1-2 weeks.
5. Blend, strain if desired, and store in the fridge.

Kombucha

Ingredients:

- 1 gallon water
- 1 cup sugar
- 4 black or green tea bags
- 1 SCOBY
- 1 cup starter kombucha

Instructions:

1. Brew tea with sugar, let cool to room temperature.
2. Pour into a large glass jar and add the SCOBY and starter kombucha.
3. Cover with a cloth and ferment for 7-14 days.
4. Bottle and ferment another 3-5 days for carbonation. Refrigerate and enjoy.

Sourdough Starter

Ingredients:

- 1 cup whole wheat flour
- 1/2 cup non-chlorinated water

Instructions:

1. Mix flour and water in a jar. Cover loosely.
2. Feed daily by discarding half and adding fresh flour and water.
3. After 5-7 days, bubbles should appear, and it should smell tangy.
4. Use for baking and keep refrigerated when not in use.

Fermented Lemon Preserves

Ingredients:

- 4 organic lemons, quartered
- 2 tbsp sea salt
- 1 cup non-chlorinated water

Instructions:

1. Pack lemons into a sterilized jar with salt.
2. Pour water to cover and press down lemons.
3. Weigh down, cover loosely, and ferment for 3-4 weeks.
4. Store in the fridge and use in cooking.

Kimchi

Ingredients:

- 1 Napa cabbage, chopped
- 1/4 cup sea salt
- 1 daikon radish, julienned
- 2 carrots, julienned
- 4 green onions, chopped
- 5 cloves garlic, minced
- 1 tbsp grated ginger
- 2 tbsp Korean chili flakes (gochugaru)
- 1 tbsp fish sauce (optional)

Instructions:

1. Salt cabbage and let sit for 2 hours. Rinse and drain.
2. Mix remaining ingredients into a paste.
3. Massage into cabbage and pack into a jar, ensuring no air pockets.
4. Weigh down and ferment for 5-7 days. Store in the fridge.

Sauerkraut

Ingredients:

- 1 medium head green cabbage, shredded
- 1 tbsp sea salt

Instructions:

1. Massage salt into cabbage until liquid forms.
2. Pack tightly into a jar, submerging in its own brine.
3. Cover loosely and ferment for 1-2 weeks.
4. Refrigerate and enjoy.

Pickled Red Onions

Ingredients:

- 1 large red onion, thinly sliced
- 1/2 cup apple cider vinegar
- 1/2 cup water
- 1 tbsp sugar
- 1 tsp salt

Instructions:

1. Boil vinegar, water, sugar, and salt.
2. Pour over onions in a sterilized jar.
3. Cool, then refrigerate for at least 1 hour before serving.

Black Garlic

Ingredients:

- Whole garlic bulbs
- A rice cooker or dehydrator (with a fermentation setting)

Instructions:

1. Place whole, unpeeled garlic bulbs in a rice cooker or dehydrator at **130–160°F (55–70°C)**.
2. Leave for **2–4 weeks**, checking occasionally.
3. The garlic will turn black, soft, and caramelized. Store at room temperature in an airtight container.

Infused Olive Oils

Ingredients:

- 2 cups extra virgin olive oil
- 1/2 cup fresh or dried herbs (rosemary, thyme, basil, etc.)
- Optional: Garlic cloves, chili flakes, citrus zest

Instructions:

1. Heat olive oil gently (do not boil).
2. Add herbs and let steep for 10 minutes.
3. Cool, strain, and store in a glass bottle in the fridge. Use within 2-4 weeks.

Herb-Infused Vinegars

Ingredients:

- 2 cups vinegar (apple cider, red wine, or white vinegar)
- 1/2 cup fresh or dried herbs (tarragon, rosemary, thyme, etc.)

Instructions:

1. Add herbs to a sterilized jar.
2. Pour vinegar over herbs and seal.
3. Store in a cool, dark place for **2–4 weeks**, shaking occasionally.
4. Strain and store in a clean bottle.

Fermented Cashew Cheese

Ingredients:

- 2 cups raw cashews, soaked overnight
- 2 tbsp lemon juice
- 1/4 cup water
- 1 probiotic capsule (or 1 tbsp sauerkraut brine)
- 1/2 tsp sea salt

Instructions:

1. Blend all ingredients until smooth.
2. Transfer to a bowl and cover loosely. Let ferment at **room temp for 24–48 hours**.
3. Taste, add seasonings (garlic, herbs, etc.), and refrigerate.

Miso Paste

Ingredients:

- 2 cups cooked soybeans
- 1/2 cup koji rice
- 1/4 cup sea salt
- 1/4 cup miso starter (or a bit of store-bought miso)

Instructions:

1. Mash soybeans and mix with koji rice and salt.
2. Pack tightly into a jar, pressing down to remove air pockets.
3. Cover with plastic wrap and weigh down.
4. Ferment in a cool, dark place for **6 months to 1 year**.

Soy Sauce Fermentation

Ingredients:

- 2 cups soybeans
- 1 cup wheat (toasted and ground)
- 1/4 cup sea salt
- 2 cups non-chlorinated water
- 1 tbsp koji starter

Instructions:

1. Cook soybeans, mash, and mix with wheat and koji starter.
2. Let ferment for **3 days** at room temperature.
3. Add salt and water, transfer to a jar, and ferment for **6 months to 1 year**.
4. Strain and store the liquid as soy sauce.

Homemade Yogurt

Ingredients:

- 4 cups milk (whole or plant-based)
- 2 tbsp plain yogurt (with live cultures)

Instructions:

1. Heat milk to **180°F (82°C)**, then cool to **110°F (43°C)**.
2. Stir in the yogurt starter.
3. Pour into a jar and incubate at **110°F** for **6-12 hours**.
4. Refrigerate and enjoy!

Kefir

Ingredients:

- 4 cups milk (or coconut milk)
- 2 tbsp kefir grains

Instructions:

1. Add kefir grains to milk in a glass jar.
2. Cover loosely and ferment at room temp for **24 hours**.
3. Strain out the grains and refrigerate the kefir.
4. Reuse grains for the next batch.

Golden Milk Paste

Ingredients:

- 1/4 cup turmeric powder
- 1/2 tsp black pepper
- 1 tsp cinnamon
- 1/2 tsp ginger powder
- 1/2 cup water
- 2 tbsp coconut oil

Instructions:

1. Heat water and turmeric in a pan, stirring to form a thick paste.
2. Add spices and coconut oil, mixing well.
3. Cool and store in the fridge for up to **2 weeks**.
4. Mix 1 tsp into warm milk for golden milk.

Bone Broth

Ingredients:

- 2–3 pounds beef, chicken, or pork bones (preferably with connective tissue and marrow)
- 1 onion, quartered
- 2 carrots, cut into chunks
- 2 celery stalks, cut into chunks
- 1 head of garlic, halved
- 1-2 tbsp apple cider vinegar
- 1-2 bay leaves
- 1 tsp black peppercorns
- Water to cover

Instructions:

1. Place the bones in a large pot or slow cooker.
2. Add the vegetables, vinegar, bay leaves, and peppercorns.
3. Fill the pot with water until the bones are fully submerged.
4. Bring to a boil, then reduce to a simmer. Skim any foam that rises to the surface.
5. Let simmer for **12–24 hours** (or longer for richer flavor) while occasionally adding more water as needed.
6. Strain the broth and discard the solids.
7. Store the broth in airtight containers in the fridge for up to a week, or freeze for later use.

Mushroom Broth

Ingredients:

- 4 cups mixed mushrooms (shiitake, cremini, porcini, etc.), chopped
- 1 onion, quartered
- 2 carrots, cut into chunks
- 2 celery stalks, cut into chunks
- 1 head of garlic, halved
- 1-2 bay leaves
- 1 tsp black peppercorns
- 4 cups water or vegetable broth

Instructions:

1. Place all ingredients in a large pot.
2. Add water or vegetable broth and bring to a boil.
3. Reduce heat to low and simmer for **45 minutes to 1 hour**.
4. Strain the broth and discard the solids.
5. Store the broth in airtight containers in the fridge for up to a week, or freeze for later use.

Fire Roasted Salsa

Ingredients:

- 4 large tomatoes
- 1-2 jalapeño peppers (adjust to desired heat)
- 1 medium onion, peeled
- 3 cloves garlic
- 1/4 cup fresh cilantro, chopped
- 1 tbsp lime juice
- 1 tsp salt

Instructions:

1. Roast the tomatoes, jalapeños, onion, and garlic over an open flame or on a grill until charred and softened.
2. Let the vegetables cool slightly, then peel the skins off the tomatoes and garlic.
3. Chop the roasted vegetables and combine them in a food processor or blender.
4. Add cilantro, lime juice, and salt to taste, and blend until smooth.
5. Store in an airtight container in the fridge for up to 1 week.

Fermented Salsa

Ingredients:

- 4 ripe tomatoes, diced
- 1/2 onion, finely chopped
- 1–2 jalapeño peppers, minced
- 3 cloves garlic, minced
- 1/4 cup cilantro, chopped
- 1 tbsp lime juice
- 1 tbsp sea salt
- 1/2 cup water

Instructions:

1. Combine tomatoes, onion, jalapeño, garlic, cilantro, lime juice, salt, and water in a bowl.
2. Pack the mixture into a clean glass jar, leaving about 1 inch of space at the top.
3. Cover the jar loosely and let it sit at room temperature for **2–4 days** to ferment.
4. Taste the salsa every day. Once it reaches the desired tanginess, seal the jar and refrigerate it.

Homemade Ghee

Ingredients:

- 2 pounds unsalted butter (preferably grass-fed)

Instructions:

1. Place the butter in a heavy-bottomed pot over medium heat.
2. Let the butter melt and begin to simmer.
3. Once the butter starts to foam, reduce the heat to low.
4. Allow the butter to cook for **15–20 minutes**, until the milk solids separate and turn golden brown at the bottom.
5. Strain the ghee through a fine mesh strainer or cheesecloth into a clean jar, leaving the solids behind.
6. Let the ghee cool before sealing the jar. Store in the fridge for up to a month, or at room temperature for several weeks.

Herb Butter Blends

Ingredients:

- 1 cup unsalted butter, softened
- 2 tbsp fresh herbs (rosemary, thyme, parsley, chives, etc.), finely chopped
- 1 clove garlic, minced (optional)
- Salt and pepper to taste

Instructions:

1. In a mixing bowl, combine softened butter with fresh herbs and garlic.
2. Season with salt and pepper to taste.
3. Mix until fully combined.
4. Store the herb butter in an airtight container in the fridge for up to 2 weeks. You can also roll the butter into logs and freeze for longer storage.

Chive Blossom Vinegar

Ingredients:

- 1 cup fresh chive blossoms
- 2 cups white wine vinegar or apple cider vinegar

Instructions:

1. Place chive blossoms in a clean glass jar.
2. Pour vinegar over the flowers, making sure they are fully submerged.
3. Seal the jar and store it in a cool, dark place for **2–3 weeks**, shaking the jar occasionally.
4. Strain out the blossoms and transfer the vinegar to a bottle.
5. Store the vinegar in the fridge or at room temperature.

Dandelion Wine

Ingredients:

- 2 cups dandelion petals (from approximately 200 dandelions)
- 1 lemon, thinly sliced
- 1 orange, thinly sliced
- 1 gallon water
- 3 cups sugar
- 1/4 tsp active dry yeast

Instructions:

1. Collect dandelion petals and place them in a large pot.
2. Add the lemon and orange slices, then pour the water over the mixture.
3. Bring the liquid to a boil, then remove it from the heat.
4. Let the mixture cool to room temperature, then stir in the sugar.
5. Once the sugar dissolves, add the yeast and stir well.
6. Cover the pot with a cloth and let it ferment for **3–5 days**.
7. Strain out the solids and transfer the liquid to a clean fermentation vessel.
8. Let the wine ferment for **3–4 weeks** before bottling.

Elderberry Syrup

Ingredients:

- 1 cup dried elderberries
- 3–4 cups water
- 1 cinnamon stick
- 3–4 cloves
- 1 tbsp fresh ginger, sliced
- 1/2 to 1 cup honey

Instructions:

1. Combine elderberries, water, cinnamon, cloves, and ginger in a pot.
2. Bring to a boil, then reduce the heat and simmer for **45 minutes**.
3. Strain the liquid, discarding the solids.
4. Stir in honey while the liquid is still warm.
5. Store the syrup in an airtight jar in the fridge for up to 2 months.

Mead

Ingredients:

- 2 lbs honey
- 1 gallon water
- 1/4 tsp yeast nutrient
- 1/4 tsp acid blend (optional)
- 1 packet mead yeast (or wine yeast)

Instructions:

1. Dissolve honey in warm water, stirring until fully combined.
2. Pour into a sanitized fermenting vessel.
3. Add yeast nutrient and acid blend (if using).
4. Sprinkle yeast over the surface of the mixture.
5. Cover loosely with a lid or airlock and ferment for **2–4 weeks** at room temperature, until bubbling stops.
6. Bottle and age for at least **3–6 months** before consuming.

Infused Spirits (Rosemary Vodka, etc.)

Ingredients:

- 750 ml vodka (or any spirit of choice)
- 2–3 sprigs fresh rosemary (or other herbs/spices)

Instructions:

1. Place the rosemary (or herbs/spices) in a sterilized jar.
2. Pour vodka over the herbs, ensuring they're fully submerged.
3. Seal and store in a cool, dark place for **1–2 weeks**.
4. Strain and bottle.
5. Enjoy straight, in cocktails, or as a gift!

Homemade Bitters

Ingredients:

- 1 cup high-proof alcohol (vodka, rum, or brandy)
- 1 tbsp dried orange peel
- 1 tbsp dried gentian root
- 1 tbsp dried cinnamon bark
- 1 tsp cloves
- 1 tsp cardamom pods
- 1 tbsp dried chamomile flowers
- Optional: 1–2 tsp sweetener (such as stevia or simple syrup)

Instructions:

1. Combine all ingredients in a sterilized glass jar.
2. Pour alcohol over the botanicals, ensuring they're fully submerged.
3. Seal tightly and shake daily.
4. Let steep for **2-4 weeks** in a cool, dark place.
5. Strain and bottle, adding sweetener if desired. Use sparingly in cocktails.

Fermented Ketchup

Ingredients:

- 4 cups tomato paste
- 1/4 cup apple cider vinegar
- 1/4 cup water
- 1 tbsp sea salt
- 1 tbsp sugar or honey
- 1/2 tsp ground mustard
- 1/2 tsp garlic powder
- 1/4 tsp ground cinnamon
- 1/4 tsp ground cloves

Instructions:

1. Mix all ingredients in a bowl until smooth.
2. Pack the mixture into a sterilized jar, leaving space at the top.
3. Cover loosely and allow to ferment for **3–5 days** at room temperature.
4. Once fermented, store in the fridge.

Homemade Worcestershire Sauce

Ingredients:

- 1 cup apple cider vinegar
- 1/4 cup tamari or soy sauce
- 1/4 cup molasses
- 2 tbsp Dijon mustard
- 1 tbsp garlic powder
- 1 tbsp onion powder
- 1 tsp ground ginger
- 1/2 tsp ground cinnamon
- 1/4 tsp ground cloves
- 1/4 tsp ground black pepper
- 1 tbsp tamarind paste
- 1 tbsp water

Instructions:

1. Combine all ingredients in a saucepan.
2. Bring to a simmer over medium heat, stirring occasionally.
3. Simmer for **15–20 minutes**, allowing the flavors to blend.
4. Cool, strain if needed, and bottle.
5. Store in the fridge for up to 6 months.

Ginger Bug Starter

Ingredients:

- 1 cup water
- 1 tbsp grated fresh ginger (with skin on)
- 1 tbsp sugar (white or brown)

Instructions:

1. Combine water, ginger, and sugar in a glass jar.
2. Stir to dissolve the sugar.
3. Cover with a cloth or loose lid and let sit at room temperature for **5–7 days**, feeding daily with 1 tbsp of sugar and 1 tbsp of grated ginger.
4. When the bug is bubbly and smells yeasty, it's ready to use for fermented sodas or kombucha!

Apple Cider Vinegar

Ingredients:

- 8–10 apples, chopped
- 2 cups sugar
- 1 gallon water
- 1/4 cup raw apple cider vinegar (with mother)

Instructions:

1. Combine apples and sugar in a large pot.
2. Add water to cover the apples.
3. Bring to a boil, then reduce heat and simmer for **30 minutes**.
4. Mash the apples and strain out the solids.
5. Add the raw apple cider vinegar and stir well.
6. Pour into a glass jar and cover with a cloth.
7. Ferment at room temperature for **3-4 weeks**, stirring daily.
8. Once the vinegar has reached the desired acidity, strain and store.

Herbal Simple Syrups

Ingredients:

- 1 cup fresh or dried herbs (lavender, mint, chamomile, etc.)
- 1 cup sugar
- 1 cup water

Instructions:

1. Combine water and sugar in a saucepan and bring to a simmer, stirring until sugar dissolves.
2. Add herbs and continue to simmer for **10-15 minutes**.
3. Remove from heat and let steep for an additional **15 minutes**.
4. Strain, bottle, and store in the fridge.

Chaga Tea

Ingredients:

- 1 tbsp chaga mushroom chunks (dried)
- 4 cups water

Instructions:

1. Add chaga to water in a pot.
2. Simmer on low for **2–3 hours**.
3. Strain and enjoy the earthy, slightly bitter tea.
4. You can re-use the chaga chunks for multiple brews.

Reishi Mushroom Tincture

Ingredients:

- 1 oz dried reishi mushrooms
- 1 pint alcohol (vodka, brandy, or rum)

Instructions:

1. Break the dried reishi mushrooms into smaller pieces.
2. Place them in a clean glass jar.
3. Pour alcohol over the mushrooms, ensuring they are fully submerged.
4. Seal the jar and store in a cool, dark place for **4–6 weeks**.
5. Shake the jar every few days to agitate the contents.
6. After the tincture has steeped, strain out the mushrooms.
7. Store the tincture in a dark glass dropper bottle.

Beet Kvass

Ingredients:

- 2 medium beets, peeled and chopped
- 1 tbsp sea salt
- 4 cups water
- 1 tbsp whey (optional, for faster fermentation)

Instructions:

1. Combine chopped beets, salt, and water in a large glass jar.
2. Add whey if using.
3. Stir well and cover loosely with a cloth or lid.
4. Let it ferment at room temperature for **3–5 days**, tasting each day until the desired sourness is reached.
5. Strain the liquid and store in the fridge. The beets can be reused for a second batch.

Pickled Garlic

Ingredients:

- 10 garlic cloves, peeled
- 1 cup white vinegar
- 1/2 cup water
- 1 tbsp sea salt
- 1 tsp sugar
- 1 tsp mustard seeds
- 1/2 tsp black peppercorns
- 1 small bay leaf

Instructions:

1. Place garlic cloves in a clean jar.
2. In a saucepan, combine vinegar, water, salt, sugar, and spices. Bring to a boil, stirring to dissolve the salt and sugar.
3. Pour the hot brine over the garlic in the jar.
4. Seal the jar and let it cool to room temperature, then refrigerate for **2-3 weeks**.
5. The garlic will continue to mellow as it sits.

Sweet Fermented Rice (Amazake)

Ingredients:

- 1 cup white rice (short-grain or glutinous rice)
- 5 cups water
- 1/4 cup koji rice (Aspergillus oryzae spores)
- 1/4 cup sugar (optional for sweeter version)

Instructions:

1. Rinse the rice and cook it in water until it is soft and sticky.
2. Allow the rice to cool to about **130°F (54°C)**.
3. Sprinkle the koji rice evenly over the rice and mix well.
4. Cover with a cloth and place it in a warm spot (about **85°F/29°C**) for **12–24 hours**.
5. After fermentation, the rice will become sweet and mushy. Add sugar to taste if desired.
6. Strain the mixture to remove excess solids or enjoy as is.

Smoked Salt

Ingredients:

- 1 cup coarse sea salt
- 1 small smoker or smoking chips (applewood or hickory works well)

Instructions:

1. Preheat your smoker according to the manufacturer's instructions.
2. Spread the salt in a shallow pan or dish.
3. Smoke the salt in the smoker for about **2–4 hours**, checking occasionally.
4. Once the desired smokiness is achieved, allow the salt to cool.
5. Store in an airtight container.

Fermented Nut Milk

Ingredients:

- 1 cup raw almonds (or cashews, hazelnuts, etc.)
- 3 cups water
- 1-2 tbsp probiotic powder (or use the contents of 1–2 capsules of a high-quality probiotic)
- 1 tsp vanilla extract (optional)

Instructions:

1. Soak the almonds in water for at least **12 hours** or overnight.
2. Drain and rinse the almonds.
3. Blend soaked almonds with 3 cups of water until smooth.
4. Strain through a nut milk bag or cheesecloth to extract the liquid.
5. Add probiotic powder to the milk and stir well.
6. Cover and let the milk ferment at room temperature for **12-24 hours**, depending on how tangy you like it.
7. Once fermented, refrigerate and consume within 3–5 days.

Wild Yeast Starter

Ingredients:

- 1/2 cup whole wheat flour (or any flour you prefer)
- 1/2 cup water (non-chlorinated)

Instructions:

1. Combine flour and water in a jar, stirring to create a thick paste.
2. Cover loosely with a cloth and leave it in a warm spot for **48 hours**.
3. Feed the starter daily by discarding half of the mixture and adding an equal amount of flour and water.
4. After a few days, you should start to see bubbles forming, and the mixture will begin to rise and fall.
5. Once it's bubbly and has a sour smell, the starter is ready for baking.

Herbal Gummy Bears

Ingredients:

- 1 cup fruit juice (choose your favorite flavor, like grape, apple, or citrus)
- 2 tbsp herbal tea (such as chamomile, lavender, or ginger)
- 2 tbsp honey or maple syrup (optional)
- 1/4 cup gelatin powder
- 1/4 tsp vitamin C powder (optional, for added health benefits)

Instructions:

1. Brew the herbal tea by steeping the herbs in 1/2 cup of boiling water for 5-10 minutes. Strain and set aside.
2. In a small saucepan, combine fruit juice, honey, and herbal tea.
3. Slowly sprinkle the gelatin powder into the mixture while stirring constantly to avoid clumping.
4. Heat the mixture over low heat until the gelatin dissolves completely.
5. Pour the mixture into silicone gummy bear molds and refrigerate for **2–3 hours** to set.
6. Once set, remove the gummies from the molds and store them in an airtight container in the fridge.

Preserved Egg Yolks

Ingredients:

- 10 egg yolks
- 1/4 cup sea salt
- 1/4 cup sugar

Instructions:

1. Carefully separate the egg yolks and place them in a shallow dish.
2. Mix the salt and sugar together in a bowl.
3. Gently coat each yolk with the salt-sugar mixture, ensuring each one is evenly covered.
4. Place the yolks back into the dish and cover them completely with the salt-sugar mixture.
5. Let them cure in the refrigerator for **5–7 days**.
6. After curing, rinse the yolks gently under cold water and pat dry.
7. Store in an airtight container in the fridge or dry them further for a firmer texture.

Infused Honey (Lavender, Cinnamon, etc.)

Ingredients:

- 1 cup honey (raw, preferably)
- 2 tbsp dried lavender buds (or your chosen herb/spice, like cinnamon sticks, rosemary, etc.)

Instructions:

1. Gently heat the honey in a saucepan over low heat, just warm enough to allow infusion.
2. Add your chosen herb or spice to the honey.
3. Let the mixture sit on low heat for about **10–15 minutes**, stirring occasionally.
4. Remove from heat and allow to cool.
5. Strain out the herbs or spices and transfer the infused honey into a jar.
6. Store in a cool, dark place.

Turmeric Pickles

Ingredients:

- 4–6 small cucumbers, sliced into rounds or spears
- 2 tbsp fresh turmeric root, grated (or 1 tbsp turmeric powder)
- 1 tbsp sea salt
- 2 cups apple cider vinegar
- 1 cup water
- 2 cloves garlic, smashed
- 1 tsp mustard seeds
- 1/2 tsp cumin seeds
- 1/2 tsp black peppercorns

Instructions:

1. Combine the vinegar, water, garlic, mustard seeds, cumin seeds, peppercorns, turmeric, and salt in a saucepan.
2. Bring to a simmer and stir until the salt dissolves and the mixture is well combined.
3. Place the cucumber slices or spears into a clean jar.
4. Pour the hot brine over the cucumbers, making sure they are fully submerged.
5. Let the jar cool, then seal and refrigerate for **3–5 days**. The pickles will get tangier with time.

Lemon Balm Oxymel

Ingredients:

- 1 cup fresh lemon balm leaves (or dried)
- 1 cup apple cider vinegar
- 1/2 cup honey

Instructions:

1. Chop the lemon balm leaves and place them in a clean jar.
2. Pour the apple cider vinegar over the leaves, ensuring they are fully covered.
3. Seal the jar and shake gently. Let it sit in a cool, dark place for **1–2 weeks**, shaking the jar once a day.
4. After the infusion period, strain the vinegar and return it to the jar.
5. Add honey to the infused vinegar and stir until the honey dissolves.
6. Store the oxymel in the fridge and use it for its medicinal benefits or as a refreshing drink, diluted with water.

Fermented Carrot Sticks

Ingredients:

- 5–6 medium carrots, peeled and cut into sticks
- 1 tbsp sea salt
- 4 cups water
- 1 garlic clove, smashed (optional)
- 1–2 tsp mustard seeds (optional)
- 1–2 bay leaves (optional)

Instructions:

1. Mix water and sea salt to create a brine, stirring until the salt dissolves.
2. Place the carrot sticks in a clean glass jar, packing them tightly.
3. Add garlic, mustard seeds, and bay leaves to the jar if using.
4. Pour the brine over the carrots, making sure they are completely submerged.
5. Cover the jar loosely and let it ferment at room temperature for **5–7 days**. Taste occasionally to ensure the desired level of fermentation.
6. Once fermented, store the carrots in the fridge, where they will continue to develop flavor.

www.ingramcontent.com/pod-product-compliance
Lightning Source LLC
LaVergne TN
LVHW081326060526
838201LV00055B/2487